Manga Drawing Books
How To Draw Manga
Basic Character
Book 2 [B/W]

Learn Japanese Manga Eyes and Pretty Manga Face

By Gala Publication

Published by:

Gala Publication

ISBN-13: 978 - 1508697091
ISBN-10: 1508697094

Table Of Content :

Toradora

Step 1

Step 2

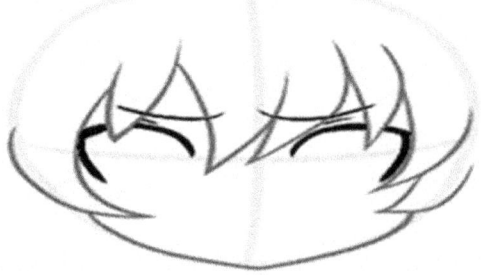

Step 3

Step 4

Step 5

Step 6

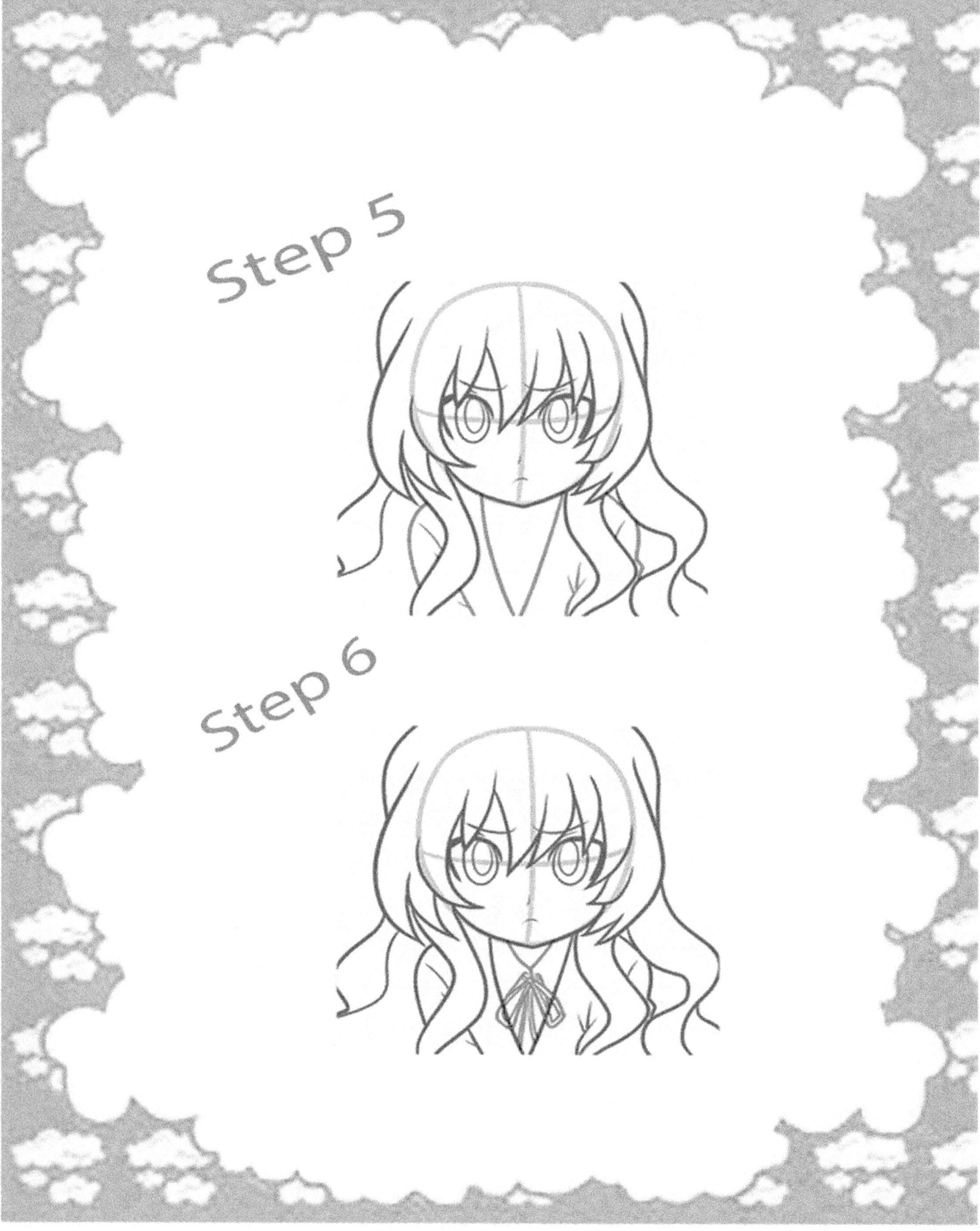

Neko

STEP 1

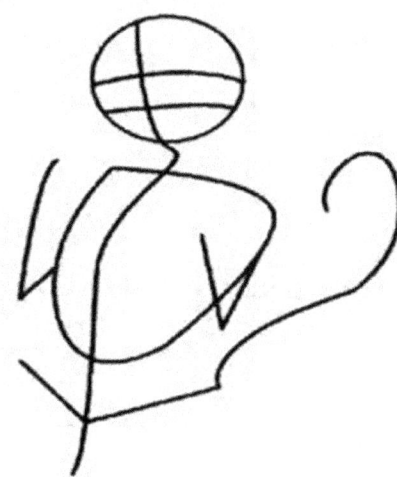

STEP 2

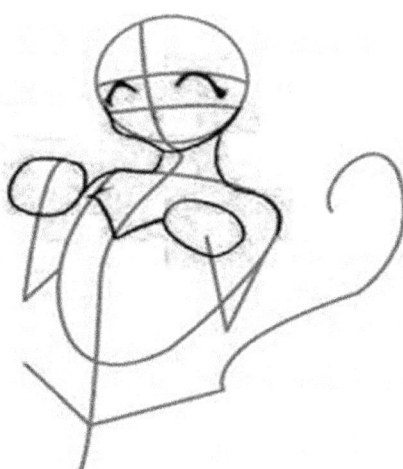

STEP 3

STEP 4

STEP 5

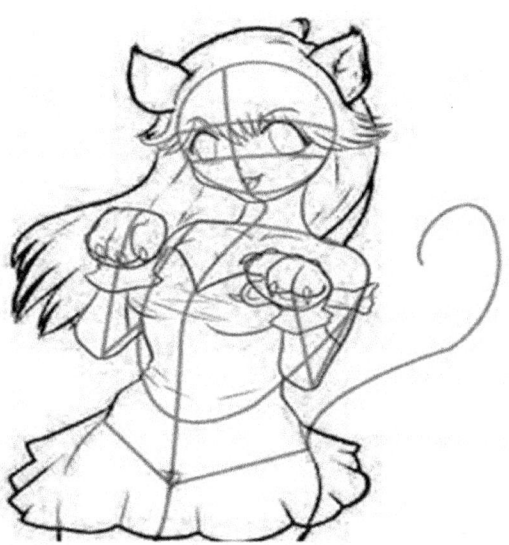

STEP 6

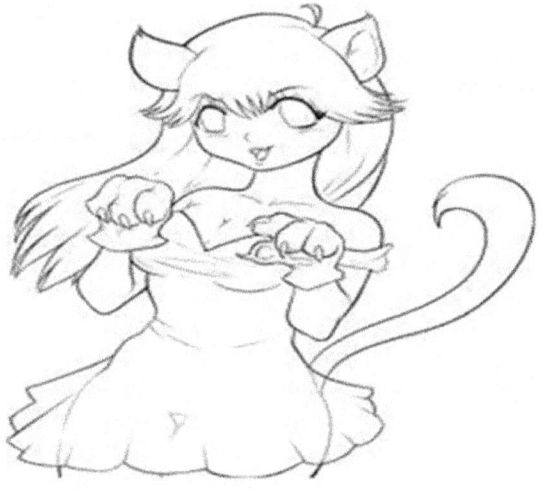

Punk - Punk - Girl

STEP 1

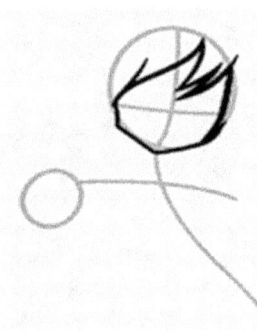

STEP 2

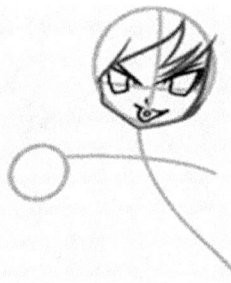

STEP 3

STEP 4

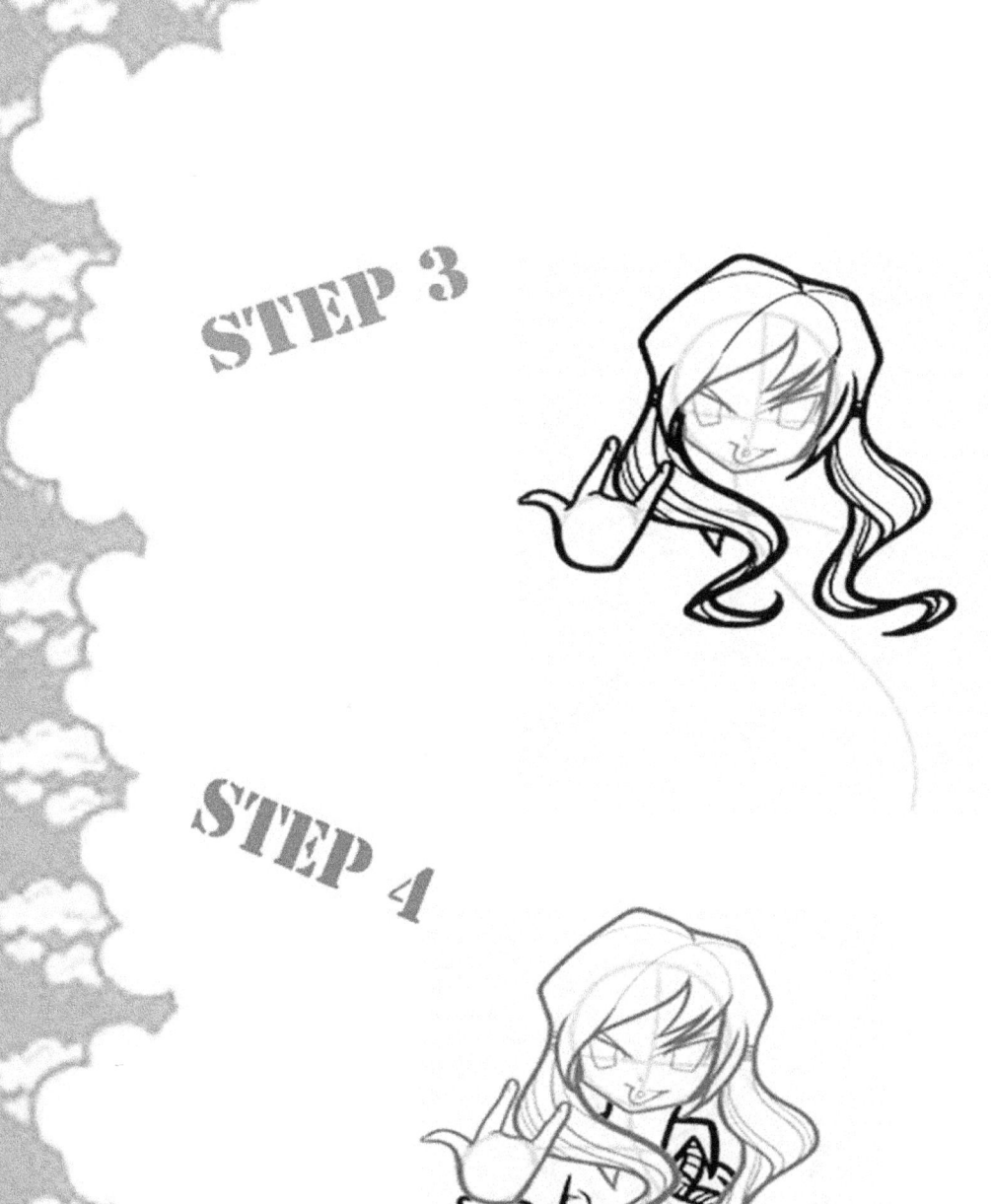

STEP 5

STEP 6

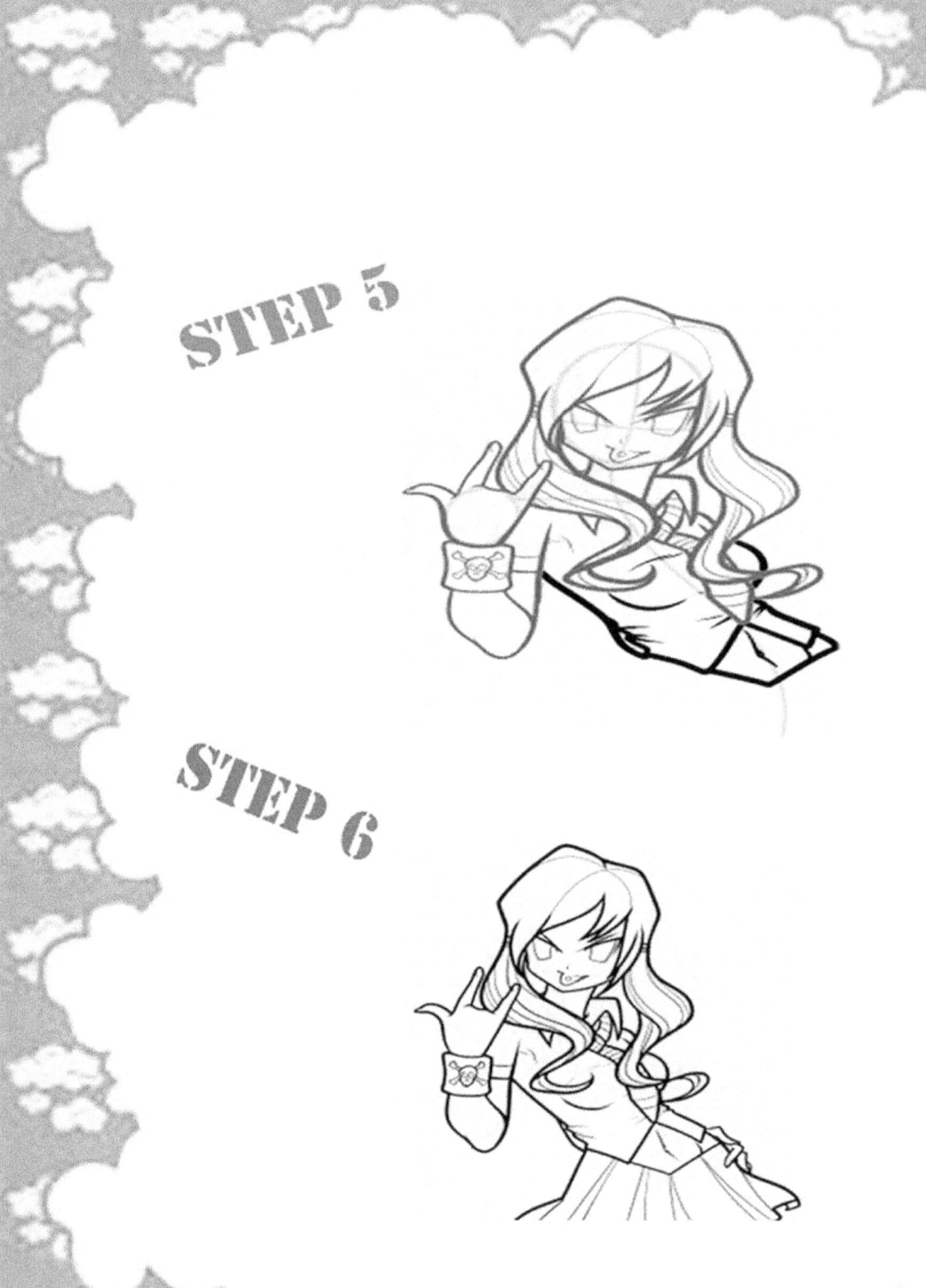

STEP 7

STEP 8

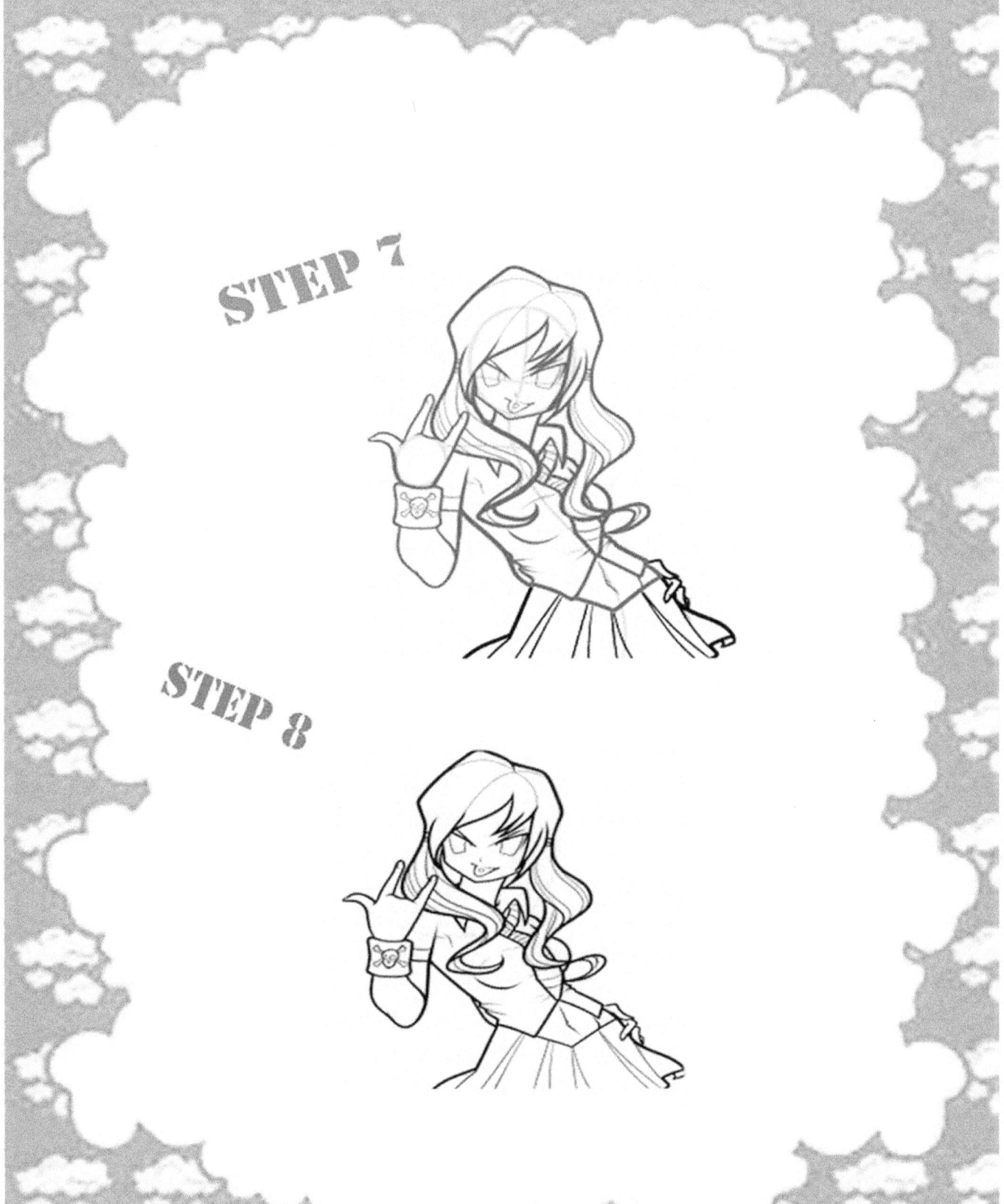

Rainbow Dash Human

Step 1

Step 2

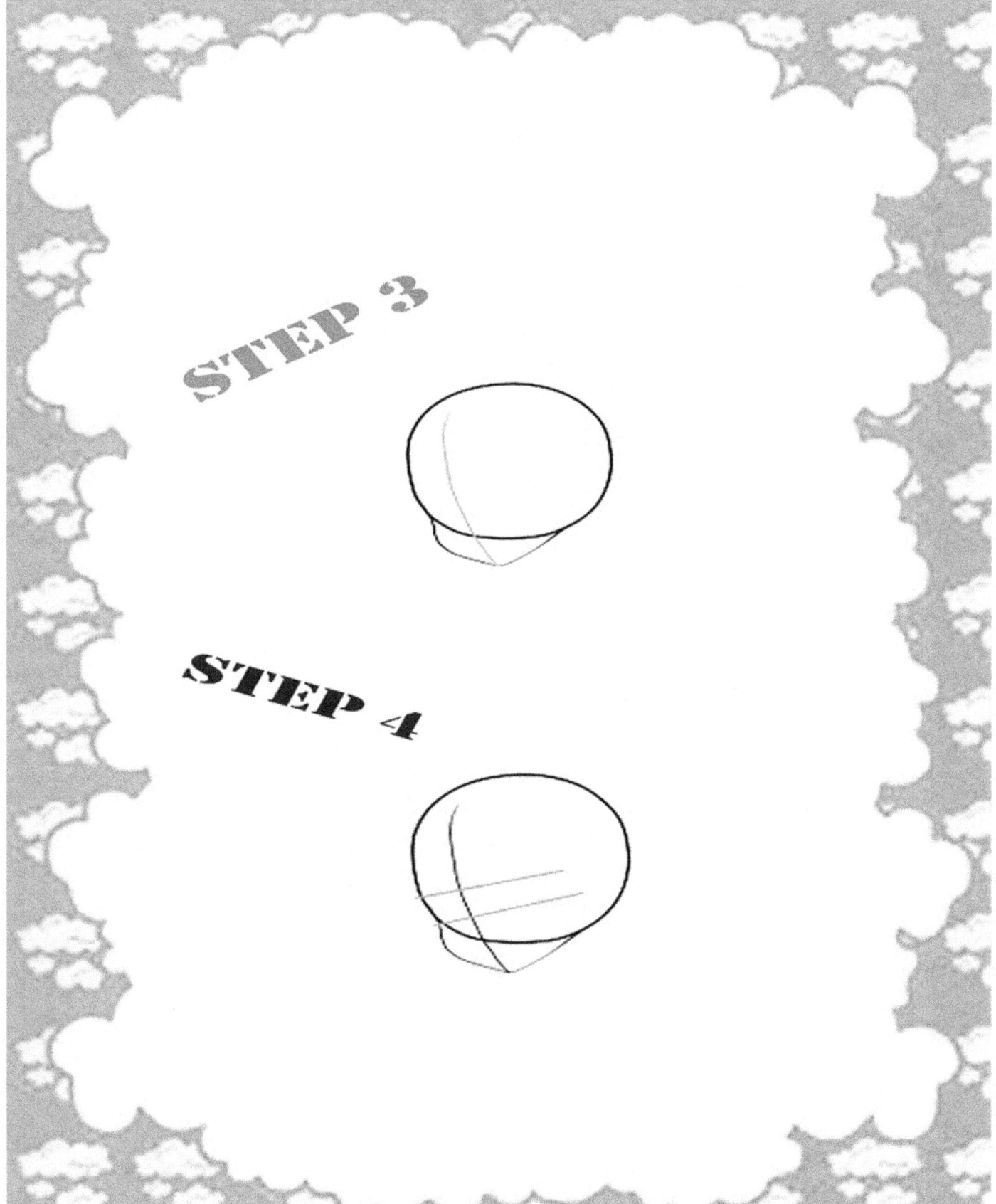

STEP 5

STEP 6

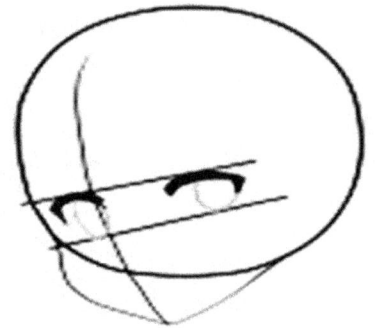

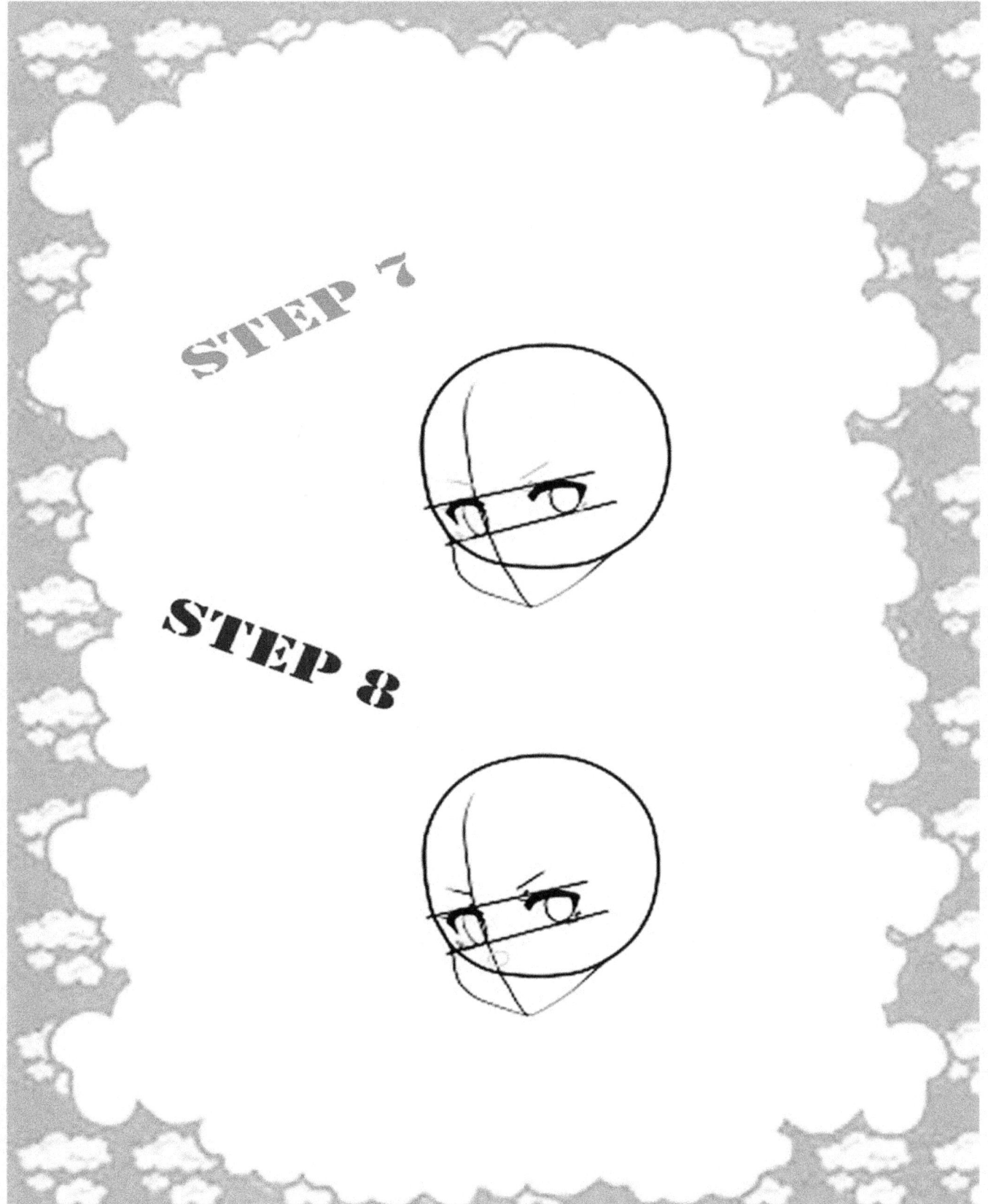

STEP 7

STEP 8

STEP 9

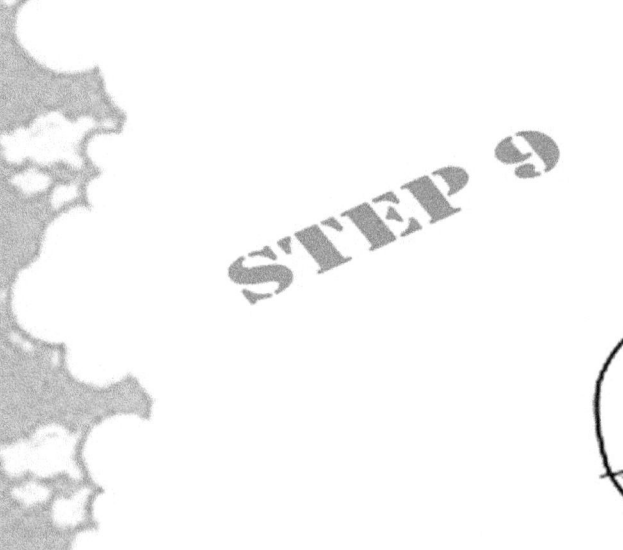

STEP 10

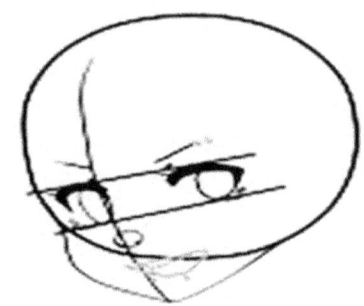

STEP 11

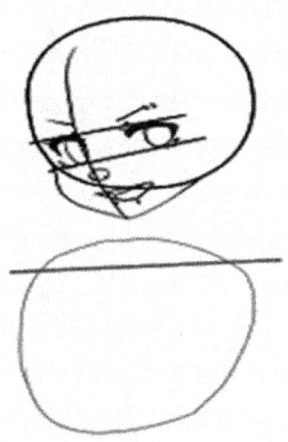

STEP 12

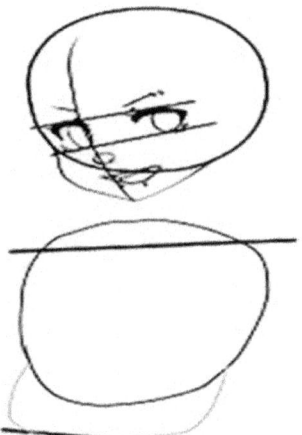

STEP 13

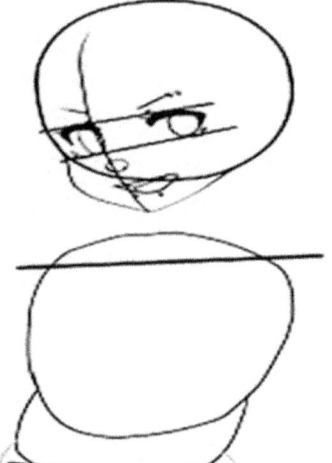

STEP 14

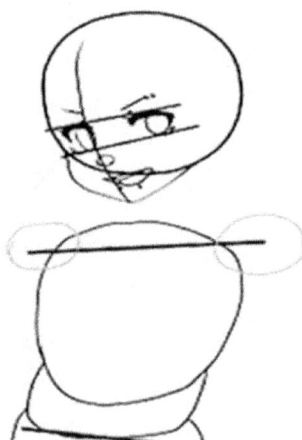

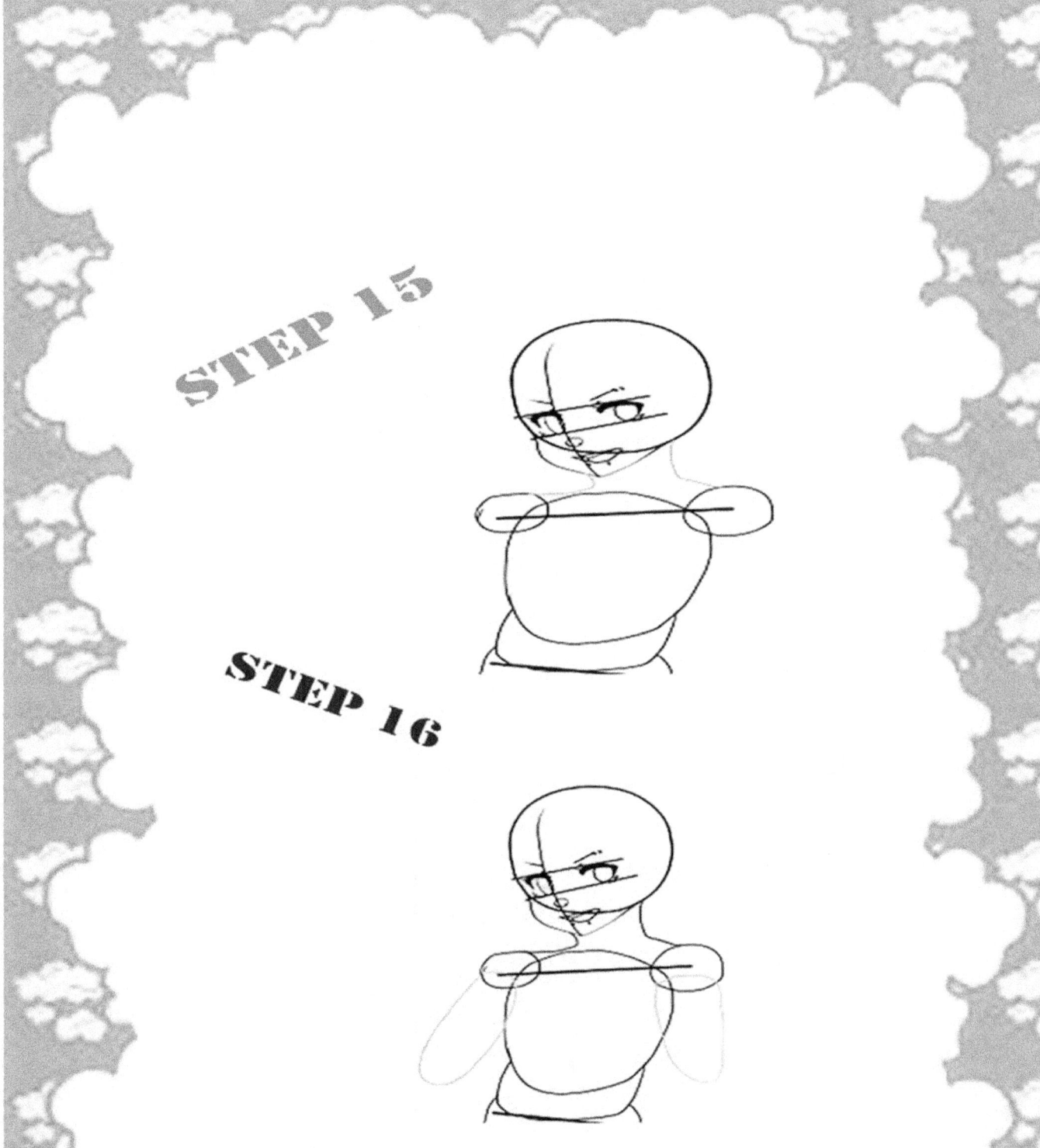

STEP 17

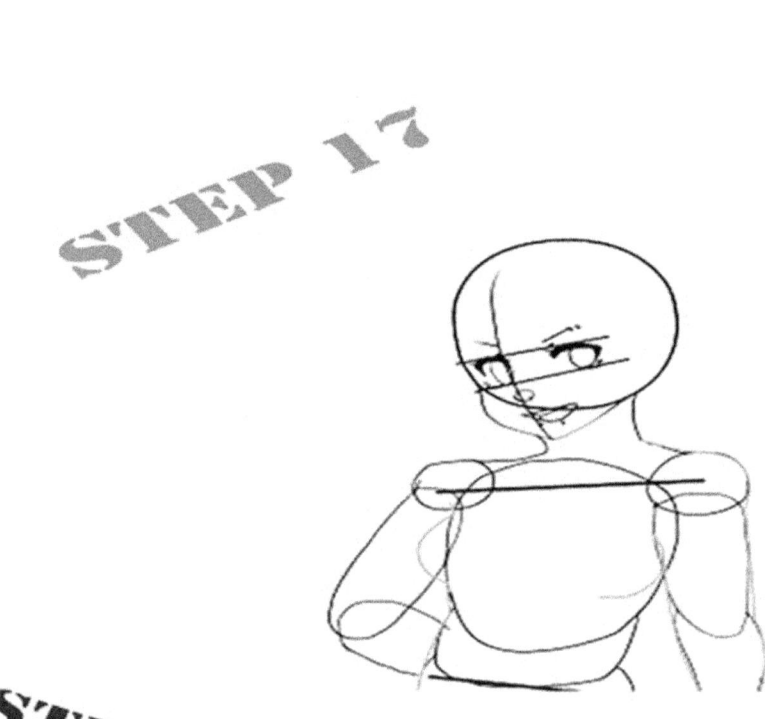

STEP 18

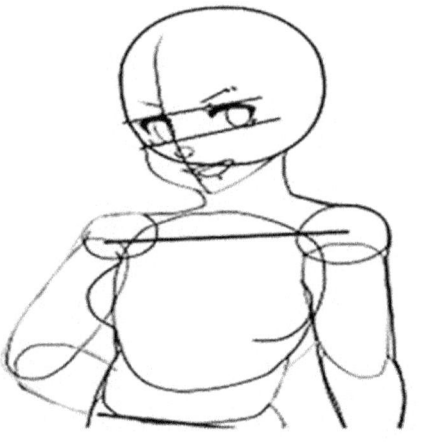

STEP 19

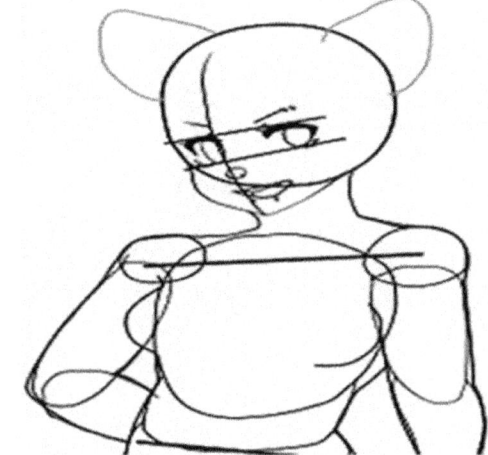

STEP 20

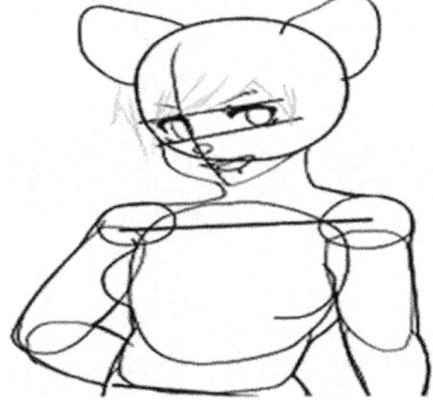

STEP 21

STEP 22

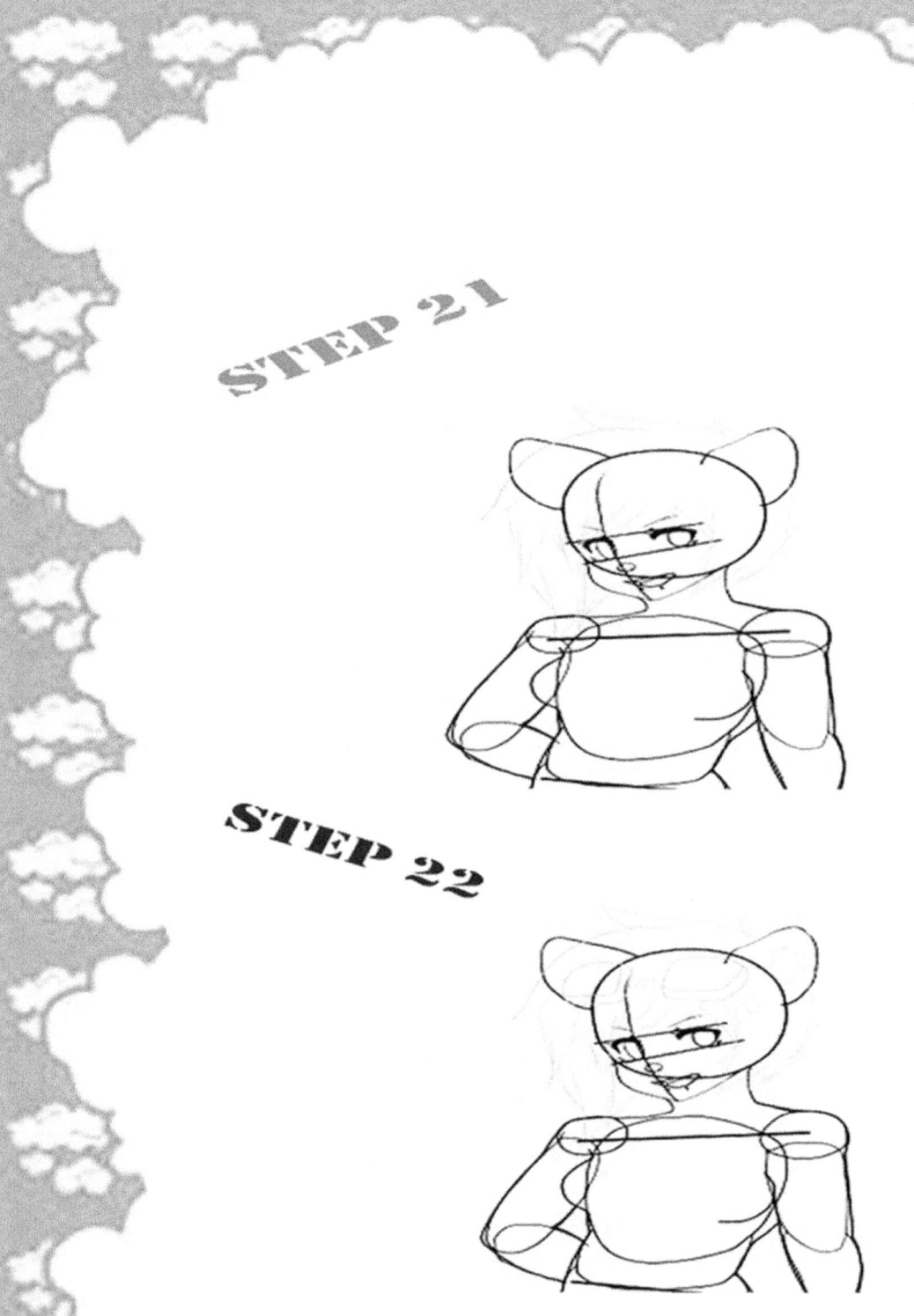

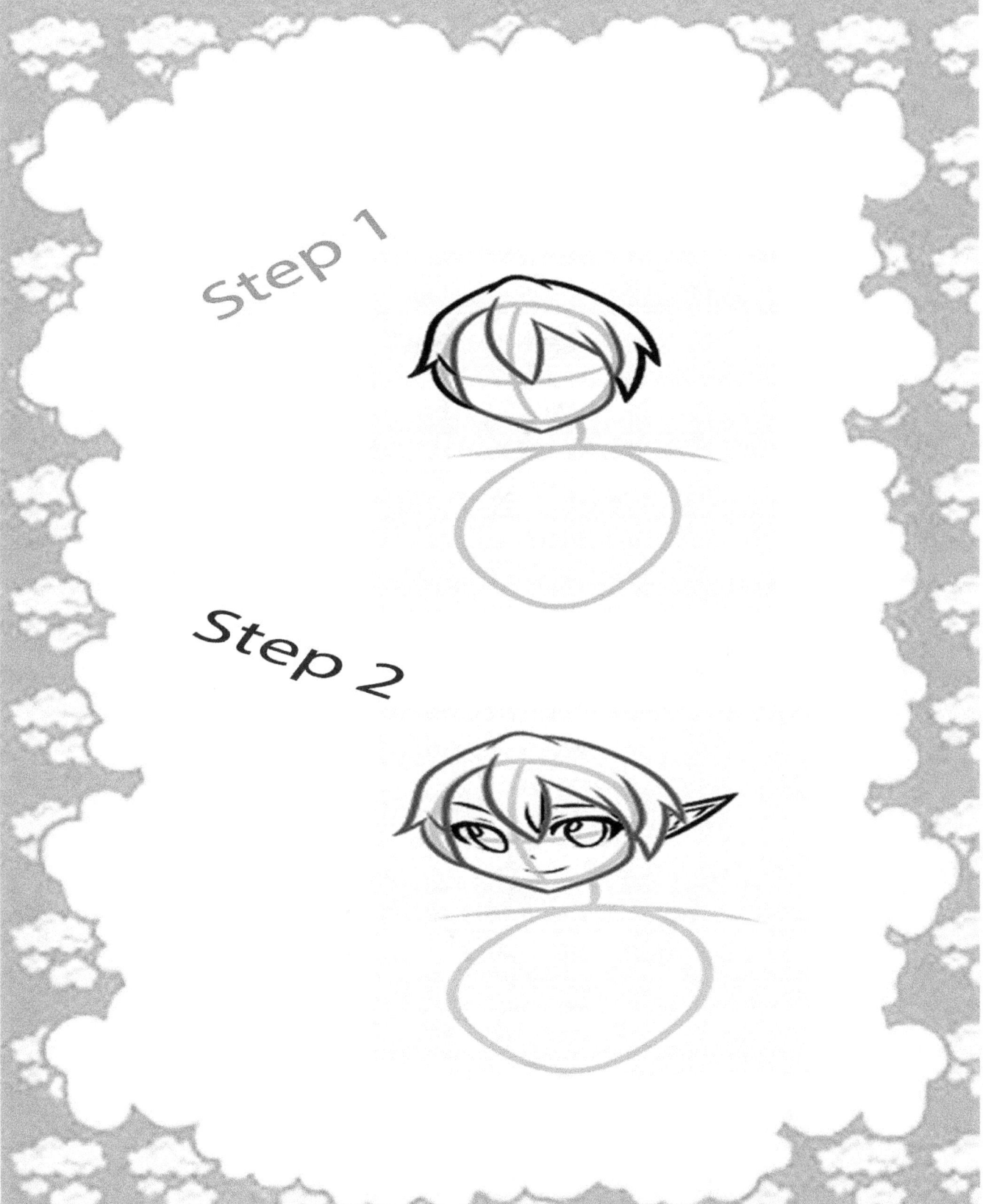

Step 3

Step 4

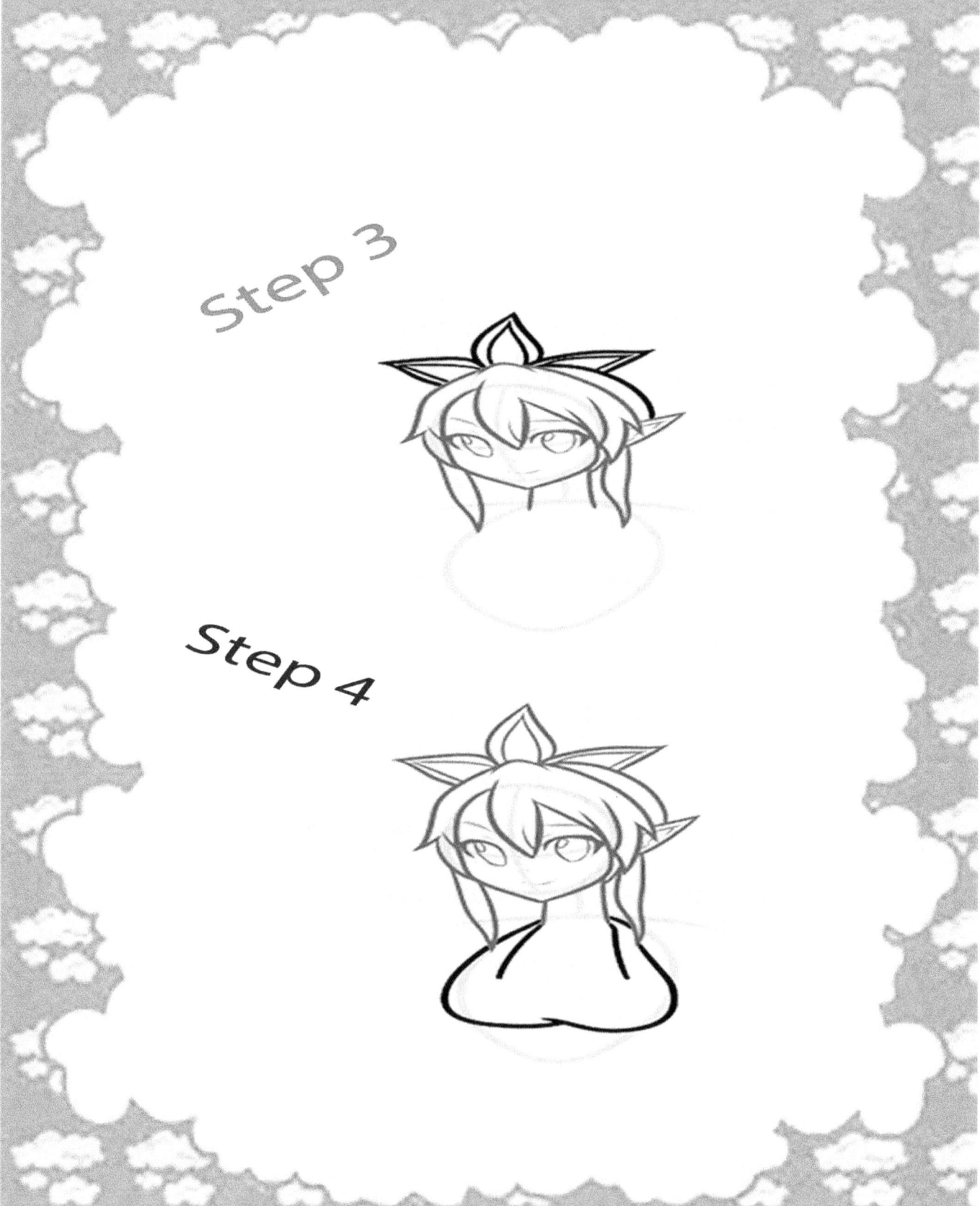

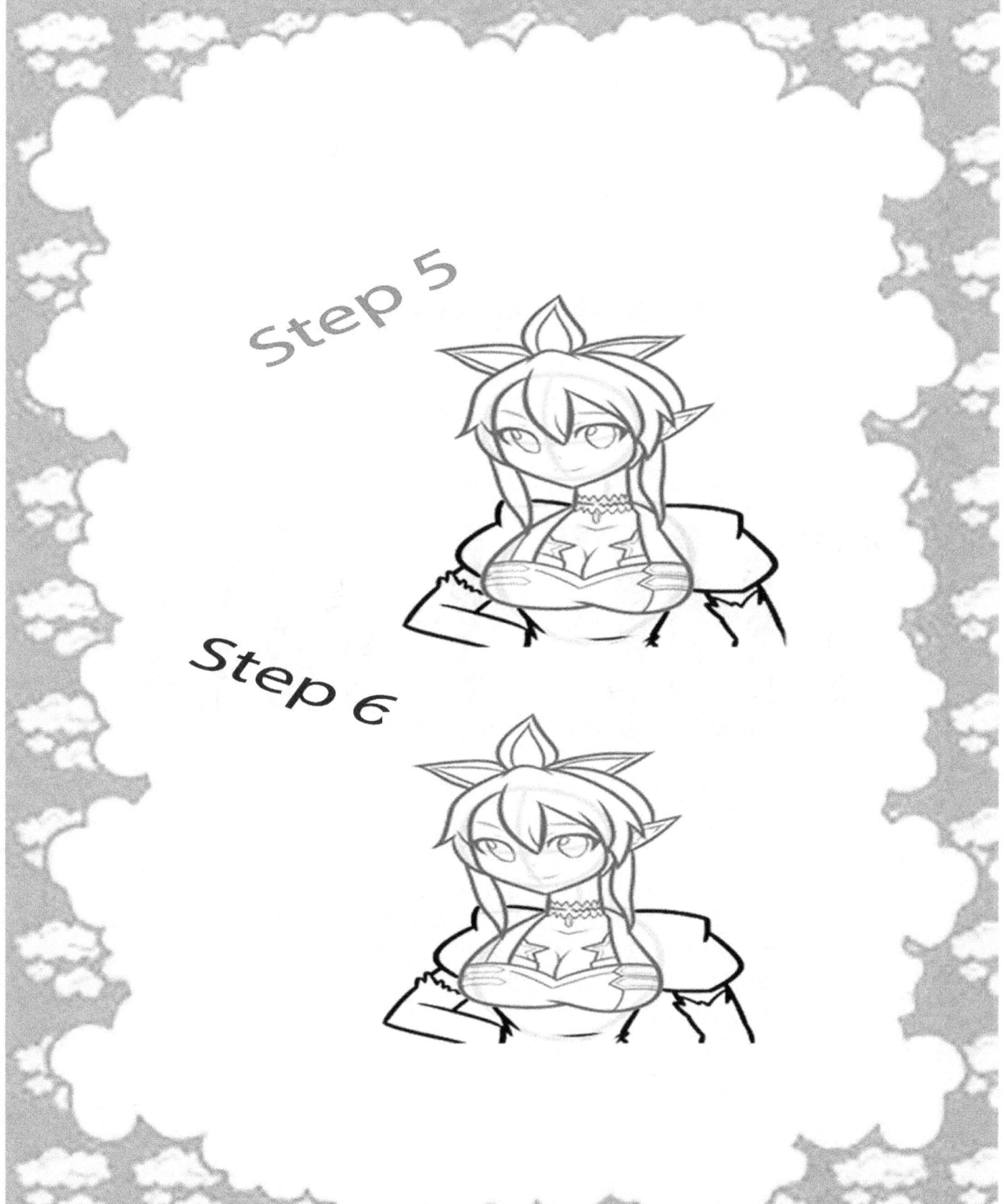

Step 5

Step 6

THE END